Toolkit #5

Developing and Marketing a Story-Telling Budget

Strategies for developing a nonprofit budget which tells a compelling story

Marilyn L. Donnellan, MS

Developing and Marketing a Story-Telling Budget

Nonprofit Toolkits
Available at
www.amazon.com/author/mldonnellan
Tool #1: Volunteer Handbooks
Tool #2: The Top Twenty Sustainability Strategies for Nonprofits
Tool #3: Becoming a Tech-Focused Nonprofit
Tool #4: ED Succession Plans & Search Process
Toolkit #5: Developing and Marketing a Story-Telling Budget

Published by CreateSpace
©2018, by Marilyn L. Donnellan, Author

All rights reserved. This includes the right to reproduce any portion of this book in any form. The author and publisher specifically disclaim any responsibility for any liability, loss, or risk, personal or otherwise, incurred consequently, directly or indirectly, of the use and application of any of the contents of this book. Although every precaution has been taken in the preparation of this book, the publisher and authors assume no responsibility for errors or omissions.

ISBN-13: 978-1720464211
ISBN-10: 1720464219

All material, figures and addendums are copyrighted and based on the books in the Nonprofit Management Simplified series, ©2017, CharityChannel Press, by M. L. Donnellan, MS

Nonprofit Management Simplified: Internal Operations, ©2017, CharityChannel Press, pg. 2

Table of Contents	Page
Introduction	4
Chapter One: The Boring Basics of why Budgets are Necessary	5
Chapter Two: How Budgets can be a Valuable Tool	10
Chapter Three: Who Develops the Budget?	15
Chapter Four: Why Budget Categories Matter	23
Chapter Five: How to Develop a Story-Telling Budget	26
Chapter Six: Strategies for Promoting Brand Identity thru the Budget	31
Chapter Seven: How to Use a Story-Telling Budget	34
Chapter Eight: Why Program Budgets are Important	38
Figures	**Page**
1: Pie Chart	5
2: Income /expense Statement	6
3: Percentage Chart	7
4: Core Elements	11
5: Planning Process	13
6: Budget Developers	16
7: Journal	19
8: Budget Trends Timeline	20
9: Budget Development Timeline	22
10: Core Mission Support	30
11: Category Comparisons	39
Addendums	**Page**
A: Administration/Finance Committee Job Description	42
B: Simplified Strategic Plan with Budget	44
About the Author	46

Introduction

Nonprofit budgets are rarely regarded as more than a necessary evil, primarily for providing a financial road map for staff, board and volunteers.

As a result, the budgets often use formats with traditional income and expense categories. Little effort is made to make the budgets anything more than a ho-hum, boring list of numbers.

But what if there was a way to have the budget tell a compelling story - one that conveys the vision and mission of your nonprofit, and which gets the reader excited about your program outcomes? The results might just cause your stakeholders to donate more of their time and money.

But how do you do that? Can you move from a boring, traditional budget format to one that tells a story and wakes up your supporters? And, what do you do with this new style of budget; how do you use it and market it?

This toolkit is a guide to all things related to budgeting, from why and how to develop budgets, and concluding with strategies to motivate you to completely re-think how budgets can be marketed to your advantage.

It is past time to re-think everything you know about budgets and your process of developing them. Wake up your budget!

Chapter One
The Boring Basics of Why Budgets are Necessary

I get it, believe me. Budgets are a necessary evil. Over the past 35 years I have developed dozens of them ranging in size from a few hundred dollars to more than six million dollars. But that's not to say they are fun or easy to develop and use.

Budgets tell a financial story. Sometimes the story is good (when income is projected to exceed expenses) and other times not so much (when the expenses exceed income).

Most budgets include a detailed list of income and expenses, based on the same old categories used for years.

Fig. 1: Pie Chart

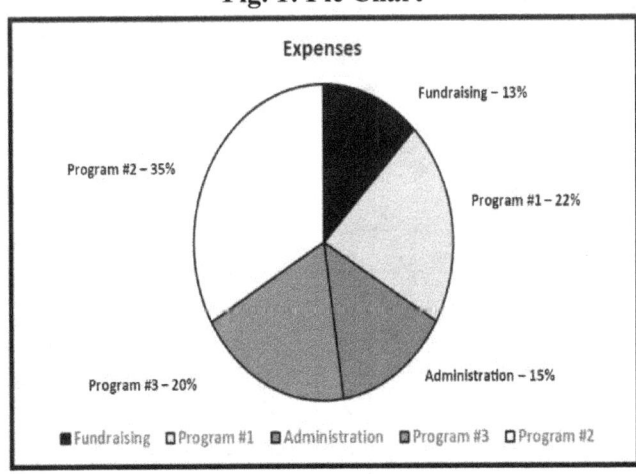

Nonprofit Management Simplified: Internal Operations, ©2017, CharityChannel Press, pg. 5

And sometimes, to negate the boring element, the executive director (ED) or accounting staff will provide a pie chart (Fig. 1), showing projected percentages for the most important areas: fundraising, administration and programs. A detailed income and expense spread sheet is the most common format (Fig. 2) and is the basis for the pie chart.

Fig. 2 Detailed Income and Expense Budget

Description	Income	%	Expenses	%	Category
Income:					
Membership fees	$165,000	9%			Programs
Client fees	$128,800	7%			Programs
United Way	$55,200	3%			Undesignated
Corporate sponsorships	$92,000	5%			Programs
Grants	$167,200	8%			Programs
Donations	$294,000	16%			Undesignated
Fund-raising events	$202,400	11%			Undesignated
Planned giving proceeds	$754,400	41%			Undesignated
Total	$1,860,000				
Expenses:					
Personnel (salaries, wages, benefits, payroll taxes)			$510,000	27%	*Spread across all categories
Program #1 – Education			$225,000	12%	Program #1
Program #1 – Counseling			$401,000	22%	Program #2
Program #3 – Court Advocate			$200,000	11%	Program #3
Rent, utilities, telephone			$73,400	4%	**Spread across all categories
Office supplies			$5,000	.03%	**Spread across all categories
Outsourcing (accounting, janitorial, website, risk management, insurance)			$20,000	1%	**Spread across all categories
Technology (equipment, upgrades, website)			$20,000	1%	**Spread across all categories
Marketing (advertising, brand identity, publicity, etc.)			$68,400	4%	**Spread across all categories
Resource Development (fundraising events, grant writing, etc.)			$276,000	15%	Resource Development
Membership fees			$1,000	.005%	*Spread across all categories
Training (including travel)			$5,000	.03%	*Spread across all categories
Contingency Fund (3% per annum for five years)			$55,200	3%	**Spread across all categories
Total			$1,860,000		

Nonprofit Management Simplified: Internal Operations, ©2017, CharityChannel Press, pg. 6

Sometimes the staff gets creative and develops a more visual representation of percentage categories (Fig. 3). But the problem with all these formats is there is no way to show how core mission goals and values are impacted by the budget.

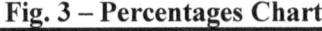
Fig. 3 – Percentages Chart

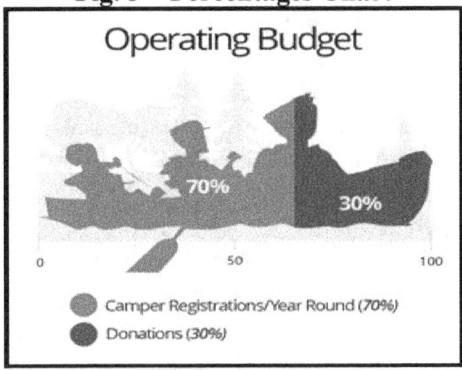

For years nonprofits have struggled with the concept of low overhead costs to meet some arbitrary percentage to show their efficient use of donor funds. Much of their budget formatting is geared to showing how low their overhead and fundraising costs are.

Too often this struggle to keep overhead costs down leads to downward spirals or starvation cycles within the nonprofits. Unable to fund basic administrative costs, simply because donors want to focus their funds on programs and not overhead, nonprofits struggle to figure out how to pay for their essential, core costs.

The reality is, if overhead costs are not fully funded, the programs will eventually fail (or starve), and the organization cannot be sustainable over the long-haul. And, not every nonprofit is going to have the same percentages of overhead costs. That's because some nonprofits, simply because of their mission, will have higher overhead costs. When they are unable to find funding for those overhead costs, they will go out of business and possibly create a big gap in community services related to their mission.

And how does this relate to the purpose of a budget? Why are budgets important? Can the issue of low overhead costs be negated? How can a budget tell a story?

Role of Budgets

First, and foremost, budgets and financial statements are public documents. This is based on the legal concept that 501(c)3 nonprofits are regarded in the United States of America by the Internal Revenue Service (IRS) as public benefit corporations. This includes governmental agencies, too. Because of that IRS designation, nonprofits are required to reveal their financial information to anyone who wants to see it.

Private, for-profit businesses have no legal obligation to reveal their budgets and financial statements. If they become public corporations, offering stocks for public trading, then they are required to make their financial information public.

Secondly, budgets and financial information are public documents because of your reporting responsibility to your stakeholders: donors, clients, volunteers, board members, staff, and the community you serve. If you are not open about your financial status, stakeholders will wonder what you are trying to hide.

Finally, issuing budgets and financial reports are a legal requirement for nonprofit boards. Boards have a fiduciary and legal responsibility to approve and monitor budgets, financial reports and audits.

But, here is where things can get dicey sometimes. If the ED and/or accounting department do not teach the board how to read and understand the budgets, financial reports and audits, they may have something to hide, or they really do not have a clue themselves about what they are supposed to be doing.

At one of the nonprofits where I served, a merger between two nonprofits, the board made the decision (before I arrived as the new CEO), to purchase a very expensive, complicated accounting software. After a year on the job, the board and I were increasingly frustrated because we could not get an accurate financial report from the accounting staff.

Their excuses were related to the complications of the merger between two nonprofits and trying to set up the new accounting system.

But then I discovered no one had trained the accounting staff on how to use the software. It wasn't until we hired qualified, trained staff were we able to get the reports we needed; a perfect illustration of what happens when the blind lead the blind. The accounting staff was blind to how to use the software, which in turn led to the CEO (me) and the board operating blind when it came to essential financial information.

Don't forget, financial statements, budgets and audits are legal documents and must be made available to the public and filed for the length of time designated by the IRS.

Chapter Two
How Budgets Can be a Valuable Tool

Budgets and financial statements can be extremely valuable tools for any nonprofits. That's because, budgets:
1. Can identify how much effort you are putting into each of the core elements (Fig. 4),
2. Should guide staff and volunteer workplans, based on the board-approved strategic planning goals,
3. Are a requirement for grant writing,
4. Along, with financial statements, reinforce your level of public accountability,
5. Are a barometer of your financial stability and long-term sustainability.

Implementation of Core Elements

When budgets are developed with income and expense categories based on each of the six core elements, for example, (administration, RD, marketing, community involvement, board and volunteer development, and programs), it is easier for the staff and volunteers to see how many resources are being channeled into each element.

If staff and volunteers focus so much time and attention on programs and resource development (RD) they ignore other essential core elements like marketing and administration, the nonprofit will suffer and not be sustainable for the long term.

Fig. 4: Core Elements of a Successful Nonprofit

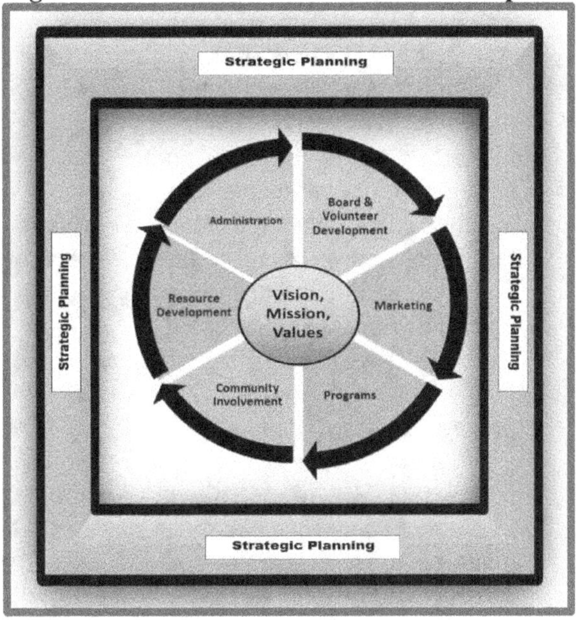

As a farm girl, I milked Bossy while I sat on a one-legged stool. The instability of the stool allowed me to move quickly if the cow decided to kick, which she frequently did.

But nonprofits must have a solid foundation, one built not just on a one-legged stool of successful programs. And this means making sure your organization's time, effort, and budgeting considers all the core elements.

Strategic Plan Development and Implementation

Secondly, budgeting is an essential part of any type of planning. There are basically four types of plans within nonprofits:

1. *A start-up plan for a nonprofit just beginning.*

The budget provides the roadmap or business plan for the basic strategies for the first year of operation.

   2. *A long-range strategic plan for 3-5 years.*

An established nonprofit can look beyond one year of planning to consider where they need to be within the next three to five years. That's because they have more historical data to use in planning. The biggest problem with long-range strategic planning, however, is the plan is usually out of date by the time the traditional planning process is completed and put into a final report. In today's fast-moving philanthropy climate, accurate long-range planning is difficult.

   3. *A simplified strategic plan for 1-2 years.*

I developed the award-winning, simplified planning process, outlined in the book, *Nonprofit Management Simplified: Board and Volunteer Development,* primarily because of the ineffectiveness and high expense of traditional long-range planning processes. The simplified planning process is greatly shortened and much more flexible, adaptable to the changing needs of the organization, if it is kept up to date. It is ideal for nonprofits new to strategic planning and small to mid-sized organizations.

   4. *Workplans for board, staff and volunteers.*

No matter how good the strategic planning process, unless it is incorporated into the workplan of all active stakeholders in the nonprofit, nothing will get done to achieve the strategic goals. And that is where implementation of the strategic plan comes into play. Fortunately, with today's plethora of great workplan software packages, there are many opportunities for you, your staff, board and volunteers to put together workable, accountable workplans to guide every core element of the nonprofit. Good planning processes will incorporate all the steps shown in Fig. 5.

Fig. 5: Strategic Planning Process

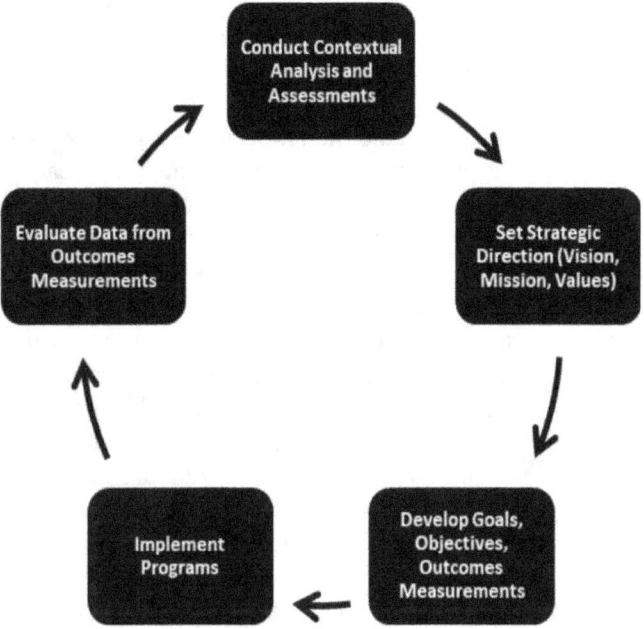

The process of developing a budget incorporates the same steps as the strategic planning process:

1. Contextual analysis and assessments of past and current budgets and their context in all the core elements,
2. Direction setting - What is the budget supposed to accomplish, based on the vision, mission and values?
3. Set goals, objectives and measurable budget outcomes
4. Implement the budget
5. Evaluate the budget data and the measurable outcomes of implementation.

Required for Grant Writing

I manage a virtual team of grant writers. One of the most frustrating aspects of the process is getting accurate and timely budget information from the clients. Why is that? Maybe it is because nonprofits do not incorporate their budget into their workplans but see it as a one-time effort prior to the beginning of the fiscal year.

It also appears the nonprofit staff often have no clue how to develop and present budgets which tell a story to potential funders and other stakeholders.

The other day I found a comic strip style diagram meant to illustrate the process of grant writing. Buried deep at the end was a very small reference to budgets. Budgets are much more important than that.

Put yourself in the shoes of a potential funder. How can you honestly consider a funding application with a boring, half-hearted, meaningless budget? Story-telling budgets are essential for successful grant writing. Donors need to know you will be accountable for how you spend their hard-earned money; budgets help you show accountability.

Accountability Tool

Too many times it is easy to blame someone else for difficulties raising adequate funds. A well-drafted budget is one of the most important tools you must have to tell the story of your mission and help you raise money. It is truly your number one accountability tool. When all your stakeholders can look at your budget and easily understand what you are trying to accomplish, you have developed a great story-telling budget.

If the financial side of your administration is visibly accountable to donors, the board, staff and the public, problems with funding and long-term sustainability will diminish.

Chapter Three
Who Develops the Budget?

I was chagrined and embarrassed to discover at the last nonprofit where I served that the co-directors of our day-care program had no clue how to develop a budget.

When I arrived in October, I had only three months to develop the next fiscal year's budget. I asked each of the directors of the many different programs to get their budgets to me by November 1st.

About a week before their budget was due, the daycare directors sheepishly walked into my office and told me they had no clue how to develop a budget. Apparently, from the time they founded the daycare, they simply operated based on the amount of income and expenses each month. In other words, if there wasn't money in the checking account, they waited until there was before paying bills.

Unfortunately, too many nonprofits operate the same way as the daycare directors: no budget and executing programs day to day based on available funds rather than on a budget. A checkbook is not a budget.

Budget Development Stakeholders

There are four main groups or individuals responsible for developing the budget. Each of these players knows, or should know, what it takes to run the programs and to develop and expand the mission.

As you can see from Fig. 6, budget development begins with the program or division directors. For example, the director of the internal operations (IO) division of the nonprofit is the best person to develop the budget for that department. In small nonprofits the person developing the IO budget might be the executive director, while in larger organizations the chief operating officer would develop it.

Fig. 6 – Budget Developers

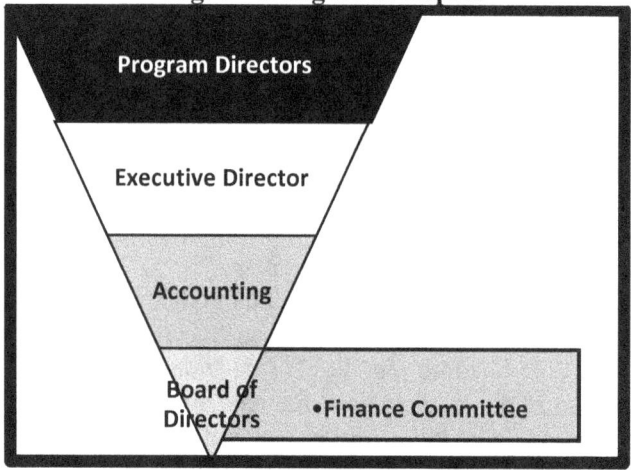

Once the program and division directors have submitted their budgets to the ED, then the ED can review it before meeting with the accounting department to complete work on the draft budget. Input from the accounting department senior staff should include comparisons to previous year's income and expenses, and projected changes in any category.

The importance of identifying marketable budget categories will be demonstrated in the next chapter.

Once the ED and senior accountant agree on the budget, it then goes to the finance committee, either a task force appointed by the administration or internal operations committee, or a standing committee appointed by the board of directors. Make sure the committee operates based on a job description (Addendum A).

Members of the committee should include some individuals with financial backgrounds, such as accountants. But include citizens without financial expertise to provide a sounding board for the understandability of the budget.

This group of volunteers can be your biggest advocates for presentation of the budget. But that will only happen if you move toward a story-telling budget they can understand and enthusiastically support.

It is helpful, too, if these volunteers have been involved in the annual strategic planning process so they know the key strategic goals the board has approved. Make sure the committee is trained in how to read budgets and financial statements. If the eyes of any volunteer glaze over when you are talking about the budget, they have not been properly educated, or the budget is boring. When that happens, they will not be your strongest advocate for budget increases.

Once the committee is enthusiastically supportive of the proposed budget, it then goes to the board of directors for approval. I always preferred the budget be presented to the board by the finance committee volunteers, rather than by me as the CEO, or by the head of the accounting department. As staff we have an obvious conflict of interest when it comes to the budget, so the volunteers are more apt to be neutral in their presentation.

Tools for Budget Development

It is critical all staff be trained on how to track their time and distribute costs into the categories the ED, accountant and finance committee finalize. As stated before, the traditional categories used for tracking staff time and expenses are administration, fundraising and program, with multiple sub-categories.

And, too often, the accounting and administrative staff lump all their time and expenses under "administration." When they do that, it inflates the overhead costs.

Very few staff work exclusively in a single program. For example, the ED will spend time on fundraising (RD), management tasks (such as board meetings), and may even help with programs at times. If the ED does not adequately account for, or log, their time into the proper categories, it will skew the actual costs for the accounting categories.

If senior staff accurately track their time in each category, then their salary, benefits and other expenses will be divided by the percentage of time spent on each responsibility.

Besides the accurate distribution of all costs across the proper categories, the previous years' financial statements showing actual income and expense in each category, is an invaluable tool for budget development. If you have decided to use different categories for the budget for this budgeting cycle, it will take time to compare previous years' costs and income to the new categories.

A sample journal for tracking time by category or core element is shown in Fig. 7. This can be done on an Excel spreadsheet or use a time-tracking software, many now available for Smart phones.

The ED can also use this type of journal to demonstrate how they are spending their time when the ED performance review is being developed.

All staff can use this type of journal to track their time. It can be a bit of a cultural shift for staff to get used to using a time-tracking tool, but it will eventually become a part of their daily responsibilities. Once they understand how the strategy will help the nonprofit tell a compelling story, they will be more apt to embrace the idea of time-journaling.

Fig. 7: Journal

Date	Description	Time	Division: Admin, Resource Development or specific program	Organizational Objective or Core Competency
9/7	Staff meeting	1.5 hrs.	Admin	Provides effective staff leadership
	Board meeting preparation	1 hr.	Admin	Provides leadership
	Phone calls to potential board members	1 hr.	Admin	Relationship builder
	Evaluated programs for strategic planning process	2 hr.	Programs	Able to implement program evaluation strategies
	Reviewed donor database and prioritized potential leadership givers for contact by volunteers	2	Resource Development	Skilled at resource development
	Met with staff accountant regarding first audit; did internal audit; worked on financial policies to take to the Finance Committee	2	admin	Goal #1: Administration Div. CPA do an audit Goal #2: Meet Standards of Accounting for Nonprofits

Budget Timelines and Trends

Charts like Fig. 8 are great tools for showing stakeholders the historical impact of your budget. The example shows the budget deficit and surplus for the USA government during the various terms of office from President Jimmy Carter through President George W. Bush. The chart tells a story, doesn't it?

Sometimes a chart like this can help illustrate your sustainability efforts and the overall financial health of the nonprofit, too.

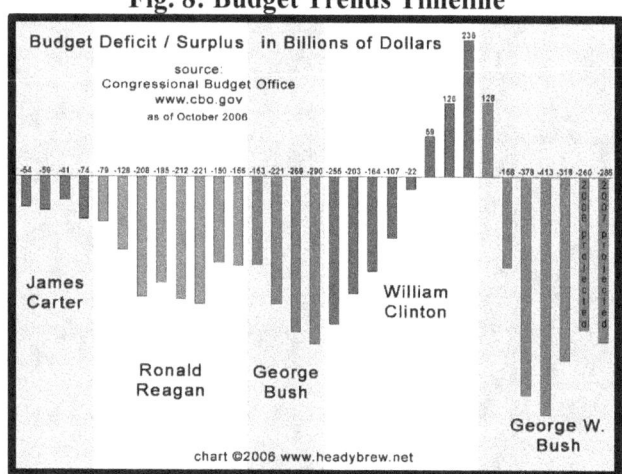

Fig. 8: Budget Trends Timeline

Use the previous years' financial statements to help you understand how to enhance the story-telling for the next year's budget. Looking at the past three to five years of financial statements can be extremely helpful in determining the future financial needs of the nonprofit.

Financial trends tell stories. If, for example, your funding from your local United Way has decreased each year of the past five, it would be important to figure out why. Is there anything you can do to turn the trend around?

The same examination of expenses is necessary. If the costs to hire qualified accounting staff have become too great, maybe you need to consider outsourcing the duties. Or, if the facility's rent costs continue to increase, maybe it is time to consider purchasing a facility or moving elsewhere. In any of these scenarios, their impact on the budget must be carefully evaluated.

Budget timelines and trends tell stories, allowing you as the ED to prove why a projected move is important, accounting should be outsourced, or efforts must be put into development of a planned giving program if the nonprofit is to be sustainable long-term.

Don't wait until one month before the end of your fiscal year to develop the next year's budget. The effort will be rushed, you could miss important trends, and you will not be able to develop the essential story-telling you need to "sell" the budget to your stakeholders.

A typical timeline for budget development could look like something like Fig. 9.

Fig. 9: Budget Development Timeline

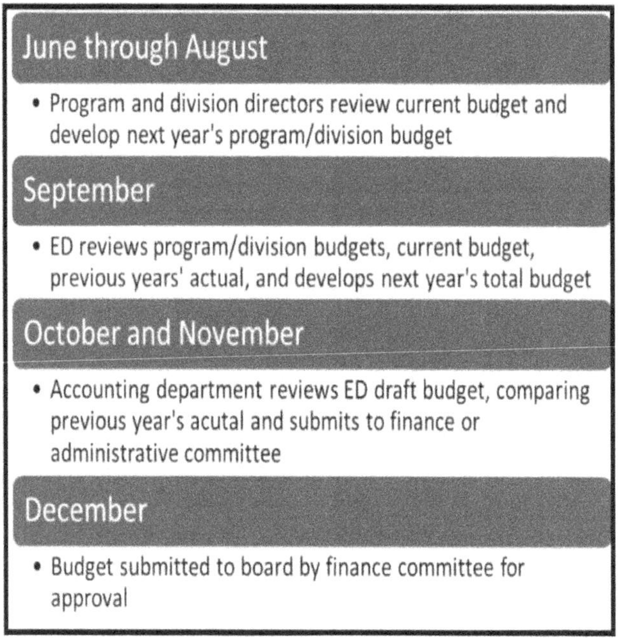
June through August
• Program and division directors review current budget and develop next year's program/division budget
September
• ED reviews program/division budgets, current budget, previous years' actual, and develops next year's total budget
October and November
• Accounting department reviews ED draft budget, comparing previous year's acutal and submits to finance or administrative committee
December
• Budget submitted to board by finance committee for approval

Nonprofit Management Simplified: Internal Operations, ©2017, CharityChannel Press, pg. 22

Chapter Four
Why Budget Categories Matter

One of the biggest challenges in nonprofit budget development is categorizing income and expenses so you are better able to tell a story. Income categories, by their very nature, are less of a problem because budget-readers can easily understand where the money is coming from. What is less understandable are expense categories.

As I said before, the old method of setting budget expense categories was to divide expenses into three basic categories: programs, RD (fundraising), and administration (overhead). Unfortunately, this has led to the starvation cycle mentioned in chapter one, with nonprofits constantly struggling to keep overhead costs down so they are more appealing to potential donors and funders.

Fortunately, that old paradigm is dying. But nonprofits still need to work hard to inform donors of the rationale for overhead costs by using a story-telling type of budget. And budget categories matter greatly in this type of budget. The big challenge for nonprofits and grant writers is to figure out how to present the budget in a story format, emphasizing outcomes and program success, rather than dollars spent in specific categories.

Why Story-Telling Narratives Matter

Budget storytelling, in its broadest sense, is about the three "c's:" collaboration, communication and connection.

When putting together the budget, collaboration with all the players outlined in the last chapter is essential: board members, accounting staff, program/division staff, etc. You must listen to what their frustrations are related to the budget, and their concerns.

Only then will you be able to address their concerns through communication of a different budget narrative. The result will be a much greater, positive connection with all the stakeholders, resulting in more available resources.

It is obvious the way we have done our budget narratives in the past is not working, since we continue to fight the overhead battle. When we develop the budget in a hurry and in isolation, we will fail to adequately convey our successes and needs. The result can be a huge disconnect with our stakeholders.

If we do our budget story-telling correctly, the programs' budgets will personalize what we are doing. This can cause potential funders to have that golden "ah-ha" moment when the light bulb goes on and they really get what we are doing and why.

And, that cannot happen if we do not have in place a solid, research-based, outcomes measurements process for every aspect of our nonprofits. There is a huge difference between telling donors how many clients you served and how you changed their lives.

Which tells a better story? "We served 500 children last year," or "If you put a child in a scouting program at a young age, the chances of them ending up on welfare or in the criminal justice system is less than one percent."

Your challenge is to figure out how to tell the donor those kinds of positive outcomes through your budget and financial statements.

Budget story-telling also tells donors what you did with their donation. If your budget emphasizes how many paper clips you purchased instead of how children were impacted, you are telling the wrong story.

The other thing a story-telling budget does is illustrate how important the core vision and mission are. This type of budget approach proves you cannot conduct effective programs without the support of the core funding (administration and fundraising). If you tell the story right, the old overhead justification struggles will go out the window for good.

Why the Right Categories are Necessary

Consider the difference in your emotional response to the two following budget categories for administrative costs:

- Overhead, or
- Core support.

The terms mean the same thing in your budget, but one (overhead) emotes a negative connotation while the other (core support) conveys a more positive reaction to the reader.

Now let's go through the steps for developing a story-telling budget, based on defining the right categories.

Chapter Five
How to Develop a Story-Telling Budget

As you would in any budget development process, you need to first itemize anticipated income and expenses, adding a minimum five percent cushion on everything except projected fixed costs, costs that will remain the same as the previous year (such as rent).

You might want to consider itemizing income and expenses based on the core elements (Fig. 4). If you educate stakeholders on the equal importance of each element, you will be able to justify expenditures in all six categories.

Or, maybe you will choose to use the traditional three categories: administration, fundraising and programs. That's fine. But be sure stakeholders know how all three are tied directly to the board-approved strategic plan and the budget implications. Addendum B shows a simplified strategic plan with a column added to identify the budget impact for each goal.

Re-define Budget Categories

Now comes the step we rarely spend enough time on: defining budget categories. Try to look at the income and expense categories in a totally different way. Terms like "fundraising" carry different emotional reactions than words like "resource development."

A creative way to develop categories is to think of your financial statement in building terms; like you were constructing a facility. In this scenario, all the income and expense categories could use building terms, like: foundation, framework, furnishings, infrastructure, etc.

Let me stop a minute and give you a reality check. You will undoubtedly run into pushback from traditional accountants and auditors who will try to tell you changing categories cannot be done, and you must use standard accounting terms. However, the same budget can be presented in a variety of formats: one for filing the IRS 990, one for an audit, and one for public consumption or marketing. Just make sure the financial information is the same in all the formats you use for the budget and financial reports.

Look for words which convey effective internal controls instead of a word like "accounting," which can be boring. Develop words to emotionally describe each program, instead of "Program #1." Program categories are where you can get creative and convey exactly what the program is about: child abuse prevention, homes for homeless, vocational training, food for children, etc.

Use Visual Tools to Promote the Budget

Curtis Klotz, CFO at Propel Nonprofits, blogged (May 2018) in The Nonprofit Quarterly on this subject of recasting budgets into visual tools. What he proposes fits neatly into this discussion of a story-telling budget.

I have adapted his chart (Fig. 10) to this concept of a story-telling budget. Notice the graphic shows three programs (outer ring) by descriptive names and defines them as "Program Specific Expenses." This refers to every expense unique to each program: books, counseling staff, training, etc.

The second ring is for program expenses shared by the programs, such as percentages of facilities costs (based on the square footage used by each program), office supplies, and the portion of support staff wages and salary/benefits, based on time-journals and amount of space in the building used by the program, etc.

For example, the ED knows via their journal they spent 10% of their time on the child abuse prevention program, 20% at court as a victim advocate and 5% in direct program assistance with victim support. The ED salary and benefits are then disbursed directly to each program based on those percentages. These expenses are regarded as shared program expenses.

The next ring represents core mission support. These are expenses like ED community involvement time, board development time, expenses for board and committee meetings, and any common expenses not program specific or which cannot be justified disbursement costs to programs by time journals. These support costs will include much of the accounting staff, technology, supplies (not program specific) and some facilities costs for common areas.

The center ring represents RD costs NOT specific to a program. If the victim advocates program conducts a fundraiser with the income and expenses attributed directly to that program, it would be itemized as RD costs within the victim advocates program budget. However, all undesignated fundraising and RD costs would be categorized in this area as "Common Mission Support: Resource Development."

The lines on Fig. 10 divide the pie into the percentage of the entire nonprofit allocation of expenses by program for each of the circles. Notice how each program must have a portion of both core mission support areas to be able to function.

The smallest circle with an arrow pointing to it represented the unfunded areas of each program. This is based on the income side of the budget. Some of our programs are more popular than others and are apt to receive more designated funding, which can lead to a deficit in funding for other programs.

As a result, significant under funding for any program bleeds into the other programs, requiring the nonprofit to come up with that deficit funding from somewhere. Funding for a program with a deficit in income means funds must be used from the other programs to pay for those costs or from undesignated funds.

The same thing applies to a deficit in funding for the core mission support areas. The money must come from somewhere. Unfortunately, these types of program deficits can lead staff to the illegal use of specified program grant funding for other programs, especially a problem if the grants are from some government agency.

In one of the nonprofits I served, I discovered soon after my arrival that the program director was doing exactly that: borrowing from one government grant to pay for the expenses in another government-funded program. Not only was it a violation of the law, but we had to scramble to repay those funds before a government audit exposed the practice and led to huge fines.

Hopefully, you can see from Fig. 10 how critical core mission support is to the overall financial health of the nonprofit. Use this type of graph to tell the budget story and to convince those who only want to support programs that the core mission support is critical to the success of their favorite program.

Fig. 10: Core Mission Support

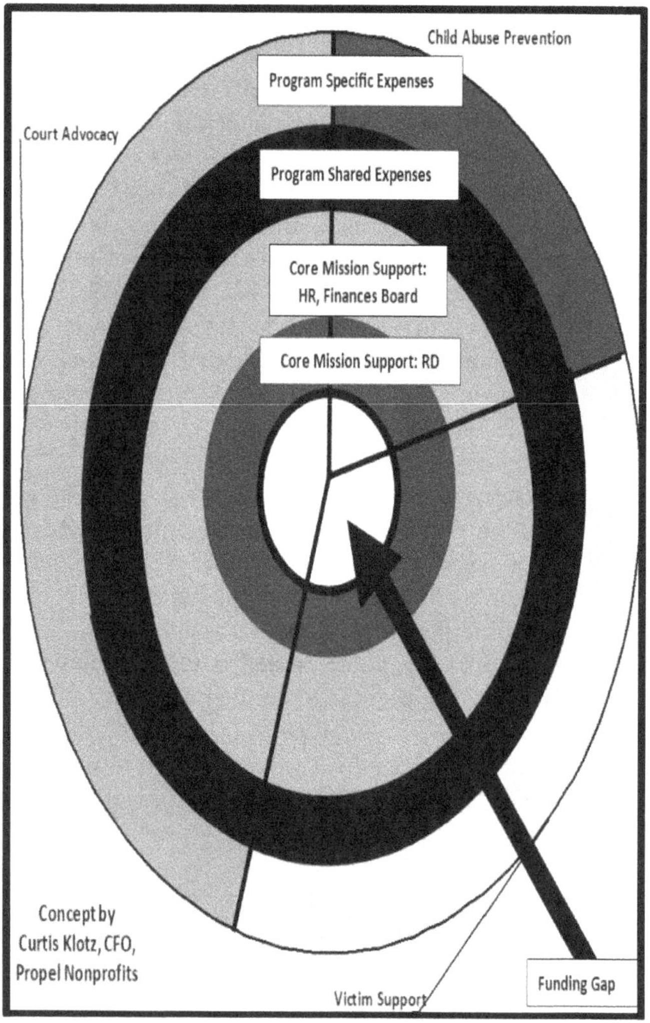

Child Abuse Prevention
Program Specific Expenses
Court Advocacy
Program Shared Expenses
Core Mission Support: HR, Finances Board
Core Mission Support: RD
Concept by Curtis Klotz, CFO, Propel Nonprofits
Victim Support
Funding Gap

Nonprofit Management Simplified: Internal Operations, ©2017, CharityChannel Press, pg. 30

Chapter Six
Strategies for Promoting Brand-Identity Thru the Budget

Story-telling budgets can be great tools for promoting your brand identity. Unfortunately, too many nonprofits have no clue what their brand identity is or how to implement brand identity strategies.

In its simplest terms, brand identity is the nonprofit's personality, vision, or how stakeholders see the nonprofit's image, good or bad. Although often associated with an expensive marketing ploy within the for-profit sector, brand identity is already attached to your nonprofit whether you realize it or not.

In 1997, Michael Treacy and Fred Wiersma wrote a book, *The Discipline of Market Leaders*. Although geared to the for-profit business, I found some exciting parallels to the nonprofit sector and have adapted some of their perspectives for building brand identity.

Treacy and Wiersma contend every business (sometimes unknowingly) is using one of three perspectives to build brand identity: operational excellence, product leadership or customer intimacy. So how do they relate to brand identity for your nonprofit, and specifically to budget story-telling?

Operational Excellence

A for-profit business who chooses an operational excellence brand strives to provide the best product in the most efficient and cost-effective way. A good example would be Amazon.

In the nonprofit sector, with an emphasis on low-cost, effective, and outstanding outcomes, The Salvation Army's substance abuse program is a great example. They have one of the lowest recidivism rates of any substance abuse program, and at the lowest cost. In this case, The Salvation Army would emphasize in their budget story-telling how low-cost and effective they are, based on proven outcomes measurements.

Product/Program Leadership

The second approach for building brand identity is that of becoming a product or program leader. Here the for-profit and nonprofit look for the newest, most innovate product or program. Cost is not an issue; creativity is. Apple is a good for-profit example of this brand,

Youth programs, like Girl Scouts, Boy Scouts and Campfire, must focus on creative programs to appeal to each new generation. In their budget story-telling, these nonprofits would be emphasizing positive outcomes and creativity not cost efficiency. In fact, as I mentioned earlier, these types of programs can prove by research results if you put a child in a scouting program at an early age, the chances of them ending up on welfare or in the criminal justice system is less than one percent.

Customer/Client Intimacy

The final approach to building positive brand identity is that of client or customer intimacy. Companies focused on this vision are determined to meet their customer/client needs, regardless of cost, even if it means referring them to someone else.

The medical and counseling professions are good examples of this strategy. In the nonprofit sector, examples include crisis hotlines like 211, information and referral programs, mental health associations and other victim advocate programs. Their budget narrative must focus on how individual client needs are being met, not on cost or creativity.

Decide which of the three approaches fits your nonprofit, if you haven't already identified your brand. All marketing strategies and budget story-telling will be based on the approach you choose.

Chapter Seven
How to Use a Story-Telling Budget

So far in our budget odyssey we have looked at the how and why of budget development, the role story-telling budgets can play in building brand identity, and strategies for putting together more effective budget stories. Now let's look at specific ways to use this kind of budget.

Workplans

Step one in developing workplans for staff and volunteers is based on the board-approved goals in the strategic plan (Addendum B) and the budget. If everyone involved understands how everything they do for the nonprofit is directly tied to the budget, they will be more apt to use funds wisely and identify funding gaps.

If the ED is not asking staff and volunteers for their input on the budget, how will they be able to happily promote the budget needs of the nonprofit through their RD efforts? Ask yourself, who does the budget belong to? You, as the ED, or to every stakeholder involved? All stakeholders should feel ownership for the income and expenses to some extent.

Tie the daily, written workplans for each staff person, volunteer, and the board to the budget. Show everyone involved how what they do impacts the budget and the story you tell. It is true that everyday duties of staff do not necessarily show up in the strategic plan as goals but be sure all those day-to-day duties are included in the written workplan.

By the way, there are great on-line tools to help everyone stay on track for the workplan, like Freedcamp and Basecamp. Some of the newer ones also incorporate the strategic planning goals into the workplan and allow board members to go online to view progress.

A good place to start in your search for the right software is: https://www.capterra.com/sem/nonprofit-software .

Case Statements

Grant writers use case statements all the time to tell the stories related to funding requests. Your budget should have a story to tell that clearly fits with the various types of case statements.

1. Vision Statement – Vision and mission statements are the basic case statements foundational to everything you do. Visions are "why" you exist and relate to the broad goal you want to accomplish. Visions drive your brand identity. For example, "All children safe from child abuse," is a vision statement.
2. Mission Statements – These case statements express "how" you plan to achieve the vision. "Preventing, educating and advocating for victims of child abuse," is a mission statement. Notice the vision statement includes no action verbs, while the mission statement does. Both vision and mission statements should be no more than 25 words and be reviewed at least every other year or during the strategic planning process. Mission drift can begin to occur when the vision and mission statement are not reviewed every few years. The simplified strategic planning process mentioned earlier incudes

strategies for reviewing your vision and mission statements.
3. Internal Case Statements – This type of case statement is usually long, very detailed and highlights all the successful outcomes of the nonprofit, including budget highlights, efficiencies, needs, etc. Marketing plans come from internal case statement, which are always based on the vision and mission statements.
4. External Case Statements – Usually a paragraph or two, these statements are always adapted to the specific funding or grant request, or to a specific audience. They are developed from the internal case statements and based on the vision and mission. When the ED speaks at the Rotary Club about the nonprofit, he/she is using an external case statement to illustrate the speech

Remember, any case statement you write must also be based on the budget narrative. Too often we write the external case statement for a grant without first asking, "what is it going to cost to execute?"

Building the budget narrative, or story, is the first step in developing internal and external case statements.

Marketing Strategies

Once you have developed a brand identity, put together your story-telling budget, and fine-tuned your case statements, you are ready to develop the marketing strategies to tell the story of your budget.

A great story-telling budget will make it easy for marketing strategies to emphasize your financial stability, accountability to stakeholders, and to implement long-term sustainability goals. How does that happen?

1. Financial stability – A story-telling budget will provide valuable information to all your stakeholders: donors, staff, volunteers, clients,

family members of clients, board members, and the public. It will also help the stakeholders understand the rationale for your income and expenses, causing them to be more knowledgeable, enthusiastic, involved, and long-term contributors. It shows them you are looking to the future and they can tell where you are headed and what it takes to get there.
2. Accountability – By showing funders how their donations are being used, it justifies your existence as a nonprofit. And, for the geeks, accountants, and folks who like the details, a story-telling budget can demonstrate the solid internal controls you have in your policies and procedures which impact every aspect of the nonprofit, not just in the accounting department.
3. Sustainability – A story-telling budget can promote a new planned giving program to provide long-term financial stability, for example. As outlined in *Toolkit #2: The Top Twenty Sustainability Strategies*, the development of long-term sustainability approaches will cause your stakeholders to understand the vision for the future and the financial roadmap it will take to get you there.

A story-telling budget is useless unless there are written workplans, case statements and effective marketing strategies to promote your brand and the budget.

Chapter Eight
Why Program Budgets are Important

I'm guessing some of you have about reached your limit when it comes to a discussion of the budget. You are ready to roll your eyes at the thought of another budgeting strategy.

But, I'm going to make it simple for you. This chapter will incorporate everything you have learned in the other chapters into the critical business of building individual program budgets.

Although I have touched on program budgets, they are so important to a story-telling budget I am going to expand on them a bit more in this chapter. Remember, when I talk about "program budgets," I am talking not just about the programs for clients, but the other aspects or divisions of your nonprofit. All the six core elements (Fig. 4) are programs or divisions of the nonprofit. "Administration," for example is a program of the nonprofit in the same way "Parent Education" is a program.

Just like the steps you take for developing the overall organizational budget, you will collect data, project income and expenses and draft a budget for each program, whether it is a service for clients, or marketing costs. However, when you build program budgets you can be much more emotional in the categories you use.

Look at Fig. 11 to see the impact using the right categories for your program budgets can have on a budget-reader's perception.

Fig. 11: Category Comparisons

Evokes Emotion	Traditional, Boring
Parent Education Supplies	Program Supplies
Victim Advocates	Volunteers
Facility Costs	Rent
Outreach	Marketing
Core Support Staff	Administration
Sustainability Income	Fundraising

Incorporating Categories into Grants

Once you have defined the categories for each program/division, developed the budgets for each, and added the outcomes information into your internal case statements, you are ready to develop the external case statements for grant writing.

One of the keys to effective grant writing is to make sure the budget narrative meets the potential funder's requirements. And, you may need to revise some program budget categories to fit the funder's verbiage.

Let's suppose you are submitting a grant to a funder whose mission is to fund parenting education programs. As a child abuse prevention nonprofit, you will use words in your budget narrative and case statements which show how your program(s) fit into their mission. Budget categories to use for this grant would include: Parent education materials, or Education workshops for parents of child abuse victims.

By simply changing the categories to fit the grant requirements, you are telling a more competing story. But how would that work for requests for administrative funding from the same funder?

One of the ways to do this is to tie the budget narrative to funder's mission: *"Our parent education program has reduced repeat abuse by 75%. However, due to a gap in funding for core mission costs for this program, such as shared administrative costs across all programs, we will be forced to reduce the number of staff in the program within six months.*

Or, *"Our positive outcomes for the parent education program (reducing repeat abuse by 75%) is a direct result of increased funding for our core mission support costs during the past year. To continue these exciting results, we are asking you for funding for the core mission support costs in the amount of $50,000."*

By focusing the case statement for the grant on the positive program outcomes, and using categories which evoke emotion, you greatly increase the changes you will be funded with a grant.

Holding Staff Accountable

It is in the program/division budgets where staff are held accountable for results. If staff has ownership for the development of their own budget, they will be less apt to overspend. Give recognition to the programs/division who come in under budget but still have outstanding, positive outcomes for clients.

Easy to do for client programs, but not so much for divisions like internal operations/administration or marketing, right? Developing outcomes measurements for every program/division of the nonprofit is essential. But how do you do it for the divisions or core elements of your nonprofit which do not seem to have clients?

First, understand that every division, program and staff person have clients; they may not realize it. For example, the clients for the accounting division would be staff and board members, since they are the ones for whom financial information is provided. But they also have secondary clients or customers, such as donors and the public.

Clients or customers are any segment of the community to which the division/program is accountable. Help the staff to identify who their customers/clients are and then look for ways to recognize efforts by staff to meet their needs.

Establishing marketing strategies

Every program/division held accountable to their clients/customers must work with the marketing division to develop strategies for promoting their positive outcomes. If the brand identity is focused on cost efficiency and organizational excellence, the administration or internal operations division would show outcomes related to the low cost per client served, the high quality internal controls which meet the Basic Standards of Accounting for Nonprofit, etc.

Program budgets provide the level of details needed to write effective grants, to hold staff accountable and to establish effective marketing strategies related to brand identity.

Budget story-telling can be a phenomenal tool for raising funds, recruiting volunteers and building sustainability. Re-think how you are putting your budget together and look for new ways to tell your stories.

Addendums

Addendum A: Job Description

Title: Administration Committee or Internal Operations Committee
Responsible to: Board of Directors
Purpose of Committee: The development of policies and monitoring of year-round internal controls for management excellence.
Key Responsibilities:
1. Planning—To develop short and long-range goals and advise the staff on action steps for goal completion
2. Resource and Needs Assessments—To assess community, volunteer, staff and internal resources available and needed to support internal operations in the most efficient and effective manner possible
3. Finance—To develop and monitor policies and procedures for internal financial management which conform to standards of accounting for nonprofits, and which meet all governmental regulations and requirements
4. Legal—To develop and monitor legal policies and procedures that conform to nonprofit laws and standards and which prevent harm to volunteers, staff and the organization
5. Facilities—To provide for the procurement, upkeep and policies related to the facilities and to assure quality facilities adequate for the completion of the nonprofit's mission
6. Technology/Equipment—To evaluate and procure equipment suitable for the efficient and

effective fulfillment of the objectives of the organization
7. Human Resources—To develop and monitor policies and procedures related to employment of staff which conform to all governmental regulations and provide for equitable treatment of employees
8. Risk Management – To annually review the insurance needs of the nonprofit and its programs; to develop safety and disaster plans and policies, and to make recommendations to the board for any additions or needed changes
9. Board Communications—To keep the board of directors informed on the implemented strategies, results of administrative efforts and any potential policies needed, that will allow for efficient and effective internal management that meets total quality management standards.

Committee Structure:
The chairman of the committee shall be a member of the board of directors and shall select, or cause to be selected, a vice chairman. The chairman and vice-chair shall also serve as members of the executive committee and shall keep the board informed on the committee's oversight of board-approved, committee goals. Most the committee shall be board members. Sub-committees or short-term task force groups may be formed to complete the committee's objectives. The treasurer and assistant treasurer shall be members of the committee.

Time Commitment:
At least one meeting per month, or as needed to fulfill the committee's goals.

Addendum B: Sample Strategic Plan with Budget

> **Sample Simplified Strategic Plan**
> **COMMUNITY CHILD ABUSE PREVENTION CENTER**
> **Vision:** All children in our community are safe from sexual abuse
> **Mission:** To educate the community, develop effective programs, and support the victims of child abuse
> **Values:** Equal treatment for all...children should be safe.... voluntarism is the best way to initiate change, etc.

MARKETING & RESOURCE DEVELOPMENT	Expenses	PROGRAMS & COMMUNITY INVOLVEMENT	Expenses
A three year-marketing plan will be developed which will increase brand identity by 30%		A community-wide collaboration of non-profits addressing similar issues will be convened within one year	
A three-year research plan will be developed which will allow for on-going responses by stakeholders and the public to brand awareness strategies		A community-wide needs and resource assessment will be developed, using the collaboration partners as stakeholders.	
Within one year all material used by the nonprofit will reflect brand identity strategies and logo.		The nonprofit will be a catalyst for the development of a community-wide plan for reducing the number of child abuse victims.	
A three-year fundraising plan will be developed which will increase financial resources by 30% per year.		Each program will develop 3-5 year plans for implementation of outcome measurement strategies within one year	
The number of grants written will increase 25% per year.		Each program will develop case statements to be used by marketing and will update them annually, based on outcomes measurements results	
A planned giving program will be established, with the first $100,000 bequest within two years.		Each program will be responsible for the development of annual budgets to be given to the ED at least one month before the annual organizational budget is due	
On-going research will identify at least one new potential fundraising market per year.		Long-term sustainability strategies will be developed for each program within one year	
Internal and external case statements will be developed and updated annually, to be used for all marketing and resource development strategies		Staff succession plans will be developed for each program	
Annual RD evaluations will show no more than 20% of funding comes from any one source		Annual program evaluations will demonstrate by research-based outcomes measurements the validity of the programs	
Annual evaluations will show expenses on all RD strategies are less than 30%		Each program will contribute client videos demonstrating successes of outcomes	

ADMINISTRATION and VOLUNTEER DEVELOPMENT	Expenses
A quality management evaluation strategy will be developed and implemented within two years.	
A plan for increasing the quality and quantity of facility space will be developed within the next year.	
A system of internal financial controls will be developed and implemented for testing by board members within one year.	
A board-level committee will research and develop suitable risk management policies and strategies.	
A detailed policies and procedures manual will be developed within two years	
A Volunteer Development Committee will be established to develop recruitment, training, recognition and dismissal policies and procedures for all types of volunteers	
A hyperlinked, on-line volunteer handbook will be developed and be available for all volunteers within one year	
A virtual volunteer plan will be implemented within two years.	
Senior staff and key volunteer succession plans will be developed within one year	
A technology and software 5-year plan will be developed, including budget, within one year	

About the Author

Marilyn L. Donnellan, MS, has more than 35 years' experience as a nonprofit CEO and consultant. The nonprofits where she served ranged in size from a single staff organization with a budget of $150,000 to a $6 million nonprofit with 300 staff. She is the author of numerous articles in nonprofit trade journals and her books on nonprofit management are in use in more than a dozen countries. She has a B.A. degree in Human Resources Management from George Fox University and an M.S. degree in Administration from Atlantic Coast Theological Seminary.

Other Books by Donnellan
Available at www.amazon.com/author/mldonnellan :
- *The Complete Guide to Church Management, (English),* Xulon Press
- *Nonprofit Management Simplified: Internal Operations,* ©2017, CharityChannel Press
- *Nonprofit Management Simplified: Board and Volunteer Development,* ©2017, CharityChannel Press
- *Nonprofit Management Simplified: Programs and Fundraising,* ©2017, CharityChannel Press
- *Nonprofit Toolkit #1: Volunteer Handbooks*
- *Nonprofit Toolkit #2: The Top Twenty Sustainability Strategies*
- *Nonprofit Toolkit #3: Becoming a Tech-Focused Nonprofit*

- *Nonprofit Toolkit #4: ED Succession Plan and Search Process*
- *Nonprofit Toolkit #5: Developing and Marketing a Story-Telling Budget*
- *Two Faces of Me* (auto-biography), Halo Press
- *Give 'til it Hurts* (fiction)

Available at www.mldonnellan.com
Training Modules *(companions to the Nonprofit Management Simplified books, and include PowerPoint, instructor notes, agenda and sample handouts)*:
- Board Development
- Effective Meetings
- Executive Director Search Process
- Grant Writing
- Internal Operations
- Risk Management
- Simplified Strategic Planning
- Sustainability
- Virtual Volunteers & Volunteers with Disabilities
- Volunteer Development
- Volunteer Handbooks

Connect with the Author
Marilyn L. Donnellan, MS
mldonnellanauthor@gmail.com
www.mldonnellan.com
www.amazon.com/author/mldonnellan

www.ingramcontent.com/pod-product-compliance
Lightning Source LLC
Chambersburg PA
CBHW030037230526
45472CB00002B/558